MY WORLD OF SCIENCE

Human Growth

Revised and Updated

Angela Royston

Heinemann
LIBRARY

H www.heinemann.co.uk/library
Visit our website to find out more information about Heinemann Library books.

To order:
☎ Phone 44 (0) 1865 888066
▤ Send a fax to 44 (0) 1865 314091
▣ Visit the Heinemann Bookshop at www.heinemann.co.uk/library to browse our catalogue and order online.

First published in Great Britain by Heinemann Library, Halley Court, Jordan Hill, Oxford OX2 8EJ, part of Pearson Education. Heinemann is a registered trademark of Pearson Education Ltd.

© Pearson Education Ltd 2003, 2008
The moral right of the proprietor has been asserted.

Editorial: Diyan Leake
Design: Joanna Hinton-Malivoire
Picture research: Melissa Allison and Mica Brancic
Production: Alison Parsons

Originated by Chroma Graphics (Overseas) Pte Ltd
Printed and bound in China by South China Printing Co. Ltd

ISBN 978 0 431 13757 5 (hardback)
12 11 10 09 08
10 9 8 7 6 5 4 3 2 1

ISBN 978 0 431 13781 0 (paperback)
12 11 10 09 08
10 9 8 7 6 5 4 3 2 1

British Library Cataloguing in Publication Data
Royston, Angela
Human growth. – New ed. – (My world of science)
  1. Human growth – Juvenile literature
  I. Title
  621.6

Acknowledgements
The publishers would like to thank the following for permission to reproduce photographs: © Corbis pp. **9** (Jim Craigmyle), **25** (Envision); © Getty Images p. **22**; © Pearson Education Ltd p. **11** (Tudor Photography); © Network/Jenny Matthews p. **21**; © Photodisc p. **7**; © Pictor International p. **23**; © Powerstock pp. **10**, **20**; © Robert Harding Picture Library p. **19**; © Science Photo Library pp. **16**, **18** (BSIP Chassenet), **28** (BSIP, LECA); © Trevor Clifford pp. **4**, **5**, **6**, **8**, **12**, **13**, **15**, **17**, **24**, **26**, **27**, **29**; unknown p. **14**.

Cover photograph reproduced with permission of © Getty Images (Stone/Sue Ann Miller).

The publishers would like to thank Jon Bliss for this assistance in the preparation of this book.

Every effort has been made to contact copyright holders of any material reproduced in this book. Any omissions will be rectified in subsequent printings if notice is given to the publishers.

O5553503   J612.6

Contents

Any words appearing in the text in bold, **like this**, are explained in the glossary.

Growing bigger

When you were born, you were a tiny baby. You grew bigger and heavier until you reached the size you are now.

You will continue to grow all the time you are a child. Sometimes you will grow faster than others. When you stop growing, you will be a "grown up"!

Changing size

Babies are different sizes when they are born. This baby is even smaller than the teddy bear. Most babies are around 50 centimetres long.

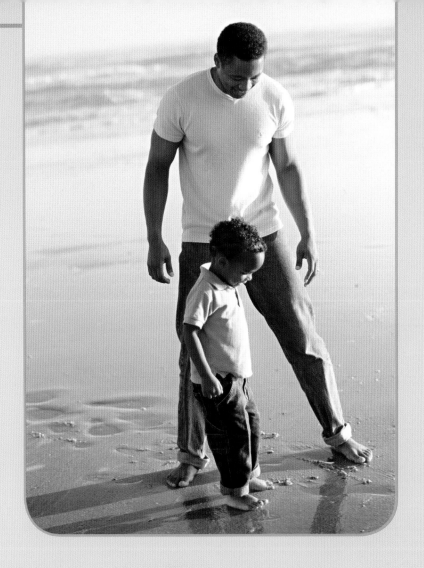

Babies and **toddlers** grow fast.
When they are three years old, most
children are more than half the
height of their **parents**.

Changing weight

As well as growing taller, you become heavier. You probably weighed about 3.5 kilograms when you were born. That is less than this bottle of water.

You weigh a lot more now. This girl is being weighed by a doctor. The doctor checks that she weighs about the right amount for her age.

Changing shape

Your body changes shape as you grow. A baby's head is big compared with the rest of its body. Its arms and legs are short.

A **toddler**'s arms and legs grow faster than the rest of its body. When you are about six years old, your legs are nearly half your **height**.

How tall will you grow?

Children grow at different rates. So some children are taller or smaller than other children. Which is the tallest child in this photo? (Answer on page 31.)

When you grow up you will probably be about the same **height** as your **parents**. If your parents are medium height, you probably will be, too.

Bones

Bones are hard and strong. They give your body its shape. Without bones, you would flop like a jelly. Your bones grow longer and thicker as you grow.

skull

ribs

arm bones

spine

fingers

thigh bone

shin bone

toes

The bones in your **spine** allow you to twist and to bend forwards and backwards. Whose spine is bending forwards the most? (Answer on page 31.)

Cells

Your body is made up of millions of different kinds of **cells**. Cells are so small that you need a special tool called a **microscope** to see them.

This is how a bone cell looks under a microscope.

Cells are like building blocks. Different parts of your body get bigger by adding on extra cells. Your body makes millions of new cells every day.

Two sets of teeth

When you were born, your first set of teeth was hidden in your **gums**. They slowly pushed through the gums. A second set formed behind them.

Your first set of teeth are called milk teeth.
They begin to fall out when you are about
six years old. The second set of teeth are
bigger. You need to look after them so that
they last the rest of your life.

Hair and nails

Hair grows faster than most other parts of your body. Some people allow their hair to grow long. Others have it cut every few months.

Nails grow quickly, too. They grow
from **cells** in the skin. This baby is
having her nails cut to stop them from
growing too long.

Healthy food

You need to drink water and eat many kinds of food. These will help you to stay healthy and grow well. Different foods help your body in different ways.

Eating food with **protein** gives you the **energy** you need to play. Your body also needs protein to grow.

Food that helps you to grow

Meat, fish, and eggs contain a lot of **protein**. Cheese and beans contain lots of protein, too. You should eat some protein food at every meal.

Bread, rice, and nuts also contain some protein. If you do not get enough protein, you will not grow very tall. Which of the foods below contain protein? (Answer on page 31.)

Food that helps your bones

These foods all help your **bones** to grow long and strong. They contain **calcium**. Calcium in your bones makes them strong.

Calcium also makes your teeth stronger.
But you still need to clean your teeth
twice a day to keep them healthy.

Thinking and learning

As children grow older, they begin to think and to learn different things. This young child is learning to use his hands as he paints.

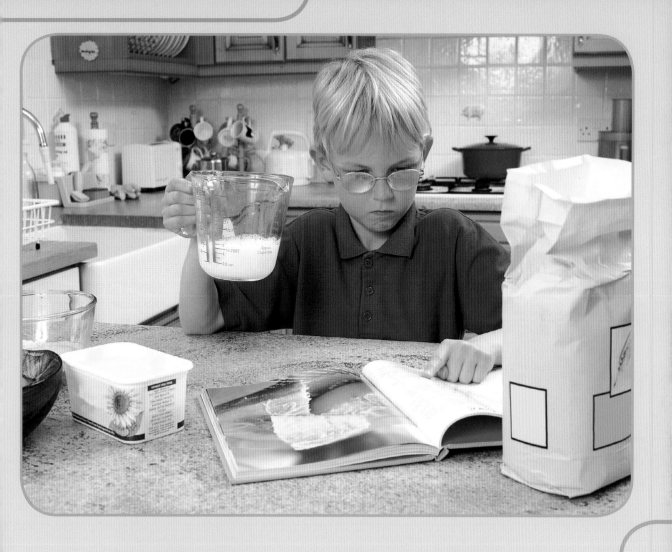

As you get older, you can do more difficult things. You also learn to read, to write, and to do maths. Your **mind** never stops growing!

Glossary

bones hard parts of the body, underneath the skin and muscles

calcium something in food that makes your bones and teeth hard and strong

cells very small building blocks that make up the different parts of the body

energy power to move and to do things

gums flesh around the teeth

healthy being well and having all the parts of the body working properly

height how tall someone is

microscope tool that allows you to look at things that are normally too small to see

mind the part of the brain that knows and thinks

parents mother and father

protein something that the body needs to build new cells. It is found in some foods.

spine back bone

toddler young child between about one and three years old

Answers

Page 12 – The girl on the left is the tallest child.

Page 15 – The spine of the girl on the right is bending forwards the most.

Page 25 – The bread, peanut butter, and rice cakes all contain protein.

More books to read

How Living Things Grow, Anita Ganeri (Heinemann Library, 2006)

My Amazing Body: A first look at health and fitness, Pat Thomas (Barron's Educational Series, 2002)

My Amazing Body: Staying Healthy, Angela Royston (Raintree, 2004)

Index